1 9 9 2

OTHER BOOKS
BY TESS GALLAGHER

Poetry

Portable Kisses

Amplitude: New and Selected Poems

Willingly

Under Stars

Instructions to the Double

Essays

A Concert of Tenses

Carver Country
photographs by Bob Adelman, introduction by Tess Gallagher

A New Path to the Waterfall
Raymond Carver, introduction by Tess Gallagher

No Heroics, Please
Raymond Carver, edited by William Stull,
introduction by Tess Gallagher

Short Stories

The Lover of Horses and Other Stories

Screenplays

Dostoevsky (with Raymond Carver)

MOON CROSSING BRIDGE

poetry by

TESS GALLAGHER

GRAYWOLF PRESS

Publication of this volume is made possible in part by a grant provided by the Min-
nesota State Arts Board, through an appropriation by the Minnesota State Legis-
lature, and by a grant from the National Endowment for the Arts. Additional sup-
port has been provided by the Jerome Foundation, the Northwest Area Founda-
tion, and other generous contributions from foundations, corporations,
and individuals. Graywolf Press is a member agency
of United Arts, Saint Paul.

Published by G R A Y W O L F   P R E S S
2402 University Avenue, Suite 203
Saint Paul, Minnesota 55114
All rights reserved.

9   8   7   6   5   4   3   2
First Printing, 1992

Library of Congress Cataloging-in-Publication Data
Gallagher, Tess.
Moon crossing bridge / Tess Gallagher.
p.   cm.
ISBN 1–55597–156–3 (cloth) : $17.00
I. Title.
PS3557.A41156M6   1992
811'.54 – dc20   91-32695

ACKNOWLEDGMENTS

Grateful acknowledgment is made to the editors and publishers of the following anthologies and periodicals, in which the poems in this collection were first published: *A Book of Women Poets from Antiquity to Now*: "Black Pudding," "Yes"; *American Poetry Review*: "After the Chinese," "Breeze," "Fathomless," "Fresh Stain," "Paradise," "Two of Anything"; *Atlantic Monthly*: "Infinite Room," "Reading the Waterfall"; *Beloit College: The Photography of Chuck Savage*: "Legend with Sea Breeze"; *Cimarron Review*: "Cherry Blossoms," "Two Locked Shadows," "Valentine Delivered by a Raven"; *Hayden's Ferry Review*: "He Would Have"; *Honest Ulsterman*: "Black Pudding," "Cold Crescent"; *Louder Than Words, A Second Collection*: "Northwest by Northwest," "Moon Crossing Bridge," "Wake," "At The-Place-of-Sadness"; *Michigan Quarterly Review*: "Black Pudding," "Ebony," "Blue Grapes"; *New Poets of the Nineties*: "Strange Thanksgiving," "Red Poppy," "Now that I Am Never Alone"; *The New Yorker*: "Now that I Am Never Alone," "Red Poppy," "Strange Thanksgiving," "Yes"; *The Paris Review*: "We're All Pharaohs When We Die"; *Parnassus*: "Quiver," "Sad Moments," "Souvenir," "Thieves at the Grave"; *Passages North*: "Cold Crescent," "Deaf Poem," "I Stop Writing the Poem"; *Poetry Canada Review*: "Ebony"; *Ploughshares*: "Black Valentine," "Magenta Valentine," "Posthumous Valentine," "Rain-soaked Valentine"; *Ploughshares Anthology*: "Ring"; *The Raven Chronicles*: "Valentine Delivered by a Raven"; *Seattle Review*: "Picking Bones"; *ZYZZYVA*: "Crazy Menu."

The author thanks Harold Schweizer who aided greatly in the preparation of this manuscript. Henry Carlile, Greg Simon, Scott Walker, Jane Mead and Tree Swenson also contributed their good help.

I thank my mother, Georgia Bond, my family and friends – as Ray would say, "They know who they are!"

Grateful acknowledgment is made to Mr. Willard Mackey for his support in the Lois Mackey Chair at Beloit College. I also received the Maxine Cushing Gray Award, an NEA Grant and a New York State CAPS Grant.

Through the gracious help of Mr. Hoji Shimanaka, President of Chuokoron-sha, my Japanese publishing house, I was able to visit Japan in November of 1990. Mr. Norio Irie, Ms. Emiko Kuroda, Mr. Shuntaro Tanikawa, and Mr. Haruki Murakami were important presences on this trip. Most important was a meeting near Kyoto with Jyakucho Setouchi, a Buddhist nun and novelist, an occasion which supported the spiritual energies behind this book's concluding work.

FOR RAY

The world is gone,
I must carry you.

PAUL CELAN

From *Poems of Paul Celan*
translated by Michael Hamburger

TABLE OF CONTENTS

I

II

III

VI

I

Furious dreams, rivers of bitter certainty,
decisions harder than the dreams of a hammer
flowed into the lovers' double cup,

until those twins were lifted into balance
on the scale: the mind and love, like two wings.
— So this transparency was built.

PABLO NERUDA

100 Love Sonnets, LIV
translated by Stephen Tapscott

YES

Now we are like that flat cone of sand
in the garden of the Silver Pavilion in Kyōto
designed to appear only in moonlight.

Do you want me to mourn?
Do you want me to wear black?

Or like moonlight on whitest sand
to use your dark, to gleam, to shimmer?

I gleam.   I mourn.

RED POPPY

That linkage of warnings sent a tremor through June
as if to prepare October in the hardest apples.
One week in late July we held hands
through the bars of his hospital bed. Our sleep
made a canopy over us and it seemed I heard
its durable roaring in the companion sleep
of what must have been our Bedouin god, and now
when the poppy lets go I know it is to lay bare
his thickly seeded black coach
at the pinnacle of dying.

My shaggy ponies heard the shallow snapping of silk
but grazed on down the hillside, their prayer flags
tearing at the void – what we
stared into, its cool flux
of blue and white. How just shaking at flies
they sprinkled the air with the soft unconscious praise
of bells braided into their manes. My life

simplified to "for him" and his thinned like an injection
wearing off so the real gave way to
the more-than-real, each moment's carmine
abundance, furl of reddest petals
lifted from the stalk and no hint of the black
hussar's hat at the center. By then his breathing stopped
so gradually I had to brush lips to know
an ending. Tasting then that plush of scarlet
which is the last of warmth, kissless kiss
he would have given. Mine to extend a lover's right past its radius,
to give and also most needfully, my gallant hussar,
to bend and take.

WAKE

Three nights you lay in our house.
Three nights in the chill of the body.
Did I want to prove how surely
I'd been left behind? In the room's great dark
I climbed up beside you onto our high bed, bed
we'd loved in and slept in, married
and unmarried.

There was a halo of cold around you
as if the body's messages carry farther
in death, my own warmth taking on the silver-white
of a voice sent unbroken across snow just to hear
itself in its clarity of calling. We were dead
a little while together then, serene
and afloat on the strange broad canopy
of the abandoned world.

CORPSE CRADLE

Nothing hurts her like the extravagance
of questions, because to ask is
to come near, to be humbled at the clotted nucleus.
One persistent cry bruises her cheekbones and she lets
it, lets the open chapel of her childhood brighten over
her with tree-light. Gray-white future
of alder, hypnosis of cedar as when
too much scent-of-nectar combs
her breathing. Rain on rain
like an upsurge in his sudden need to graze her
memory, bareheaded at the quayside
where he dreamily smoked a cigarette and guided her,
the satin shell of her stillness, toward
that same whiteness at the top of rain, swollen
and gradual. How lucid she is,
blurred edgeless, like listening
to be more wide awake, that music she pressed into him
in order to fascinate what beautifully
he had begun. All bird and no recall, she
thinks, and lives in his birdness, no burden
but strange lightness so she wants to be up at dawn,
the mountains fogged with snow, a world
that sleeps as if it were
all the world and, being so, able to be seen
at its beginning, freshly
given as sleep is, bleak fertility of sleep when
she thinks far into his last resting
wherein she drifted, drifts, slow and white,
deeply asking, deep with its dark below.

READING THE WATERFALL

Those pages he turned down in peaks
at the corners are kerchiefs now, tied
to the last light of each favorite tree
where he paused, marking my path
as surely as if he'd ordered squads
of birds to rustle leaves overhead.

And I do look up often, musing into
his warmed-over nests or letting
a thrum of recognition pulsate *koto*-like
as if his head were over my shoulder
in a cool fog allowed to think its way
down a marble staircase shorn
of its footfalls. In a child's crude
pea-pod canoe my amber beads float seaward
like a cargo meant to be lost.

How often I am held alive by half-a-matchstick,
remembering his voice across rooms
and going when called to hear some line
of poetry read aloud in our two-minded way
like adding a wing for ballast and
discovering flight.

So much of love is curved there
where his pen bracketed
the couplet mid-page, that my unused
trousseau seems to beckon deeply
like a forehead pressed into paradox
by too much invitation.

He lets me dress hurriedly for the journey
as a way to better leave me what vanishes
according to its readiness, as he is ready and glides now
into my long bedside Sunday
until we are like the dead pouring water
for the dead, unaware that our slender thirst
is unquenchable.

TRACE, IN UNISON

Terrible, the rain. All night, rain
that I love. So the weight of his leg
falls again like a huge tender wing
across my hipbone. Its continuing—the rain,
as he does not. Except as that caress
most inhabited. Ellipsis of
eucalyptus. His arms, his beautiful
careless breathing. Inscription
contralto where his lips graze
the bow of my neck. Muslin half-light.
Musk of kerosene in the hall, fixative
to ceaselessly this rain, in which
there is nothing to do but be happy, be
free, as if someone sadly accused
came in with their coat soaked through
and said, "But I only wanted
to weep and love," and we rolled toward
the voice like one body and said
with our eyes closed, "Then weep, then
love." Buds of jasmine threaded through
her hair so they opened after dark,
brightening the room. That morning
rain as it would fall, still
falling, and where we had lain,
an arctic light steady
in the mind's releasing.

BLACK PUDDING

Even then I knew it was the old unanswerable form of beauty
as pain, like coming onto a pair of herons
near the river mouth at dawn. Beauty as when the body
is a dumb stick before the moment – yet goes on,
gazes until memory prepares a quick untidy room
with unpredictable visiting hours.
So I brought you there, you who didn't belong, thinking to outsave
memory by tearing the sacred from

its alcove. I let you see us, arms helplessly tender,
holding each other all night on that awkward couch
because our life was ending. Again and again
retelling our love between gusts of weeping.
Did I let you overhear those gray-blue dyings?
Or as I think now, like a Mongol tribesman did I stop the horse
on its desert march, take the meal of blood

from its bowed neck to be heated. This then is my black pudding
only the stalwart know to eat. How I climbed
like a damp child waking from nightmare to find
the parents intimate and still awake.
And with natural animal gladness, rubbed my face
into the scald of their cheeks, tasting salt
of the unsayable – but, like a rescuer who comes too late, too
fervently marked with duty, was unable to fathom

what their danger and passage had been for. Except
as you know now, to glimpse is intrusion enough,

and when there is nothing else to sustain, blood will be thickened
with fire. Not a pretty dish.
But something taken from the good and cherished beast on loan to us,
muscled over in spirit and strong enough to carry us
as far as it can, there being advantage
to this meagerness, unsavoriness that rations itself
and reminds us to respect even its bitter portion.
Don't ask me now why I'm walking my horse.

Now that I Am Never Alone

In the bath I look up and see the brown moth
pressed like a pair of unpredictable lips
against the white wall. I heat up
the water, running as much hot in as I can stand.
These handfuls over my shoulder—how once
he pulled my head against his thigh and dipped
a rivulet down my neck of coldest water from the spring
we were drinking from. Beautiful mischief
that stills a moment so I can never look
back. Only now, brightest now, and the water
never hot enough to drive that shiver out.

But I remember solitude—no other
presence and each thing what it was. Not this raw
fluttering I make of you as you have made of me
your watch-fire, your killing light.

Legend with Sea Breeze

When you died I wanted at least to ring
some bells, but there were only clocks
in my town and one emblematic clapper
mounted in a pseudo-park for veterans.
If there had been bells I would have
rung them, the way they used to sound
school bells in the country so children
in my mother's time seemed lit
from the other side with desire
as they ran in from the fields
with schoolbooks over their shoulders.
Once more a yellow infusion of bells

empties like a vat of canaries into
the heart so it is over-full and
the air stumbles above rooftops, and death
in its quicksilver-echo shakes
our marrow with a yellow, trilling
silence. I would have given you that,
though these nightshift workers,
these drinkers in childless taverns, these mothers
of daughters seduced at fourteen — what
can the language of bells say to them
they haven't known first as swallows
blunting the breastbone? No, better

to lead my black horse into that grove
of hemlock and stand awhile. Better
to follow it up Blue Mountain Road
and spend the day with sword ferns,
with the secret agitations of creaturely

forest-loneliness. Or to forage
like a heat-stunned bear
raking the brambles for berries and thinking
only winter, winter, and of crawling
in daylight into the beautiful excess of earth
to meet an equal excess of sleep.
Oh my black horse, what's

the hurry? Stop awhile. I want to carve
his initials into this living tree.
I'm not quite empty enough to believe he's gone,
and that's why the smell of the sea
refreshes these silent boughs, and why
some breath of him is added if I mar the ritual,
if I put utter blackness to use
so a tremor reaches him as hoofbeats, as
my climbing up onto his velvet shoulders
with only love, thunderous sea-starved love,
so in the little town where they lived
they won't exaggerate when they say
in their stone-colored voices

that a horse and a woman flew down
from the mountain, and their eyes looked out
the same, like the petals of black pansies
schoolchildren press into the hollow
at the base of their throats as a sign
of their secret, wordless invincibility.
Whatever you do, don't let them ring any bells.
I'm tired of schooling, of legends, of
those ancient sacrificial bodies dragged to death
by chariots. I just want to ride my black horse,
to see where he goes.

SOUVENIR

It is good to be unused, whole as discovery —
the alabaster egg with its giant stirring.
At first, with the heat gone out of me
I thought his moon-life had lifted everything
from reach, even roses, those vermilion climbers
that were a shout at hope, up and up
my haggard trellis. But goodness
has so many silent children whose spell
lifts anchors to vessels of rock and azure, and we
go happily under our black mantle
with a tingling inside as those who live close
to the weather delight in the plain grammar
of ice, of wind over fresh tracks
through the empty valley.

So she put on her birdskin moccasins
and went out to possess her island, making sure
the tide was at ebb. Drawn by doves, she
went out with his sickle over her
in the paradise-field of stars. Wet stones
that loved with their whole being are legion
on her shore. How blackly they shine, singed and frenzied
with memory, their birth-sheen
holding on. She would throw them all back
to add intention like that proud mouth
who, in mourning, saved her drinking
only for fountains. Lucina she calls herself
under his crown of candles, Lucina with her wedding cake
crumbled into the sea. What has she saved? Rue
and red ribbon, a wreath made of tail feathers.

As with her, an early death has left its pagan mark
so everything turns to worship or sign
and I am never more alone
than when our twin gold rings come together
in a perfect chime, addressing us in the familiar
lost-future tense. I stroke her glistening hair
as he stroked mine, absently, the way candlelight licks
the night clean until one of us is gone
or disheveled into a second soul.

I I

If we believe in the soul, then perhaps
we have more in common with the dead
than the living.

JEFF KELLER

from a letter

EMBERS

He was suffering from too much light
the way our afternoons recover from
morning rain by slicing the room
in half. I read to him to bring a voice
sideways, to touch him more, and join
our listening or laughter or mutual derision.
To be one and none. Sometimes a rhyme can
snuff its substance, yet release
a second lasting. To speak aloud at a grave
breaks silence so another heat
shows through. Not speaking, but the glow
of that we spoke.

Two of Anything

What silk-thin difference is there
if I stay to dream or go.
                            KYOKO SELDEN

That small tug, which at first seems
all on its own in the strait,
can eventually be seen to pull two barges, each
twice its size, because water
understands everything and all
day says "pass, pass by." I propose
a plan and we discuss it. I'm afraid I'll never
be happy again. "Bring me
a glass of water," he says. "Someone, you know,
has to stay here and take care of things."
Two ducks fly by. I take
a few sips from his glass. Outside it's
deep blue morning, almost purple
it's so glad to be cheating
the sleepers of its willful drifting, the tangled
blue of night and the blue premonition
that will dissolve and carry
it. Two boys vicious with news fling
the morning paper house to house
down the hill. Two horses out of childhood I loved,
Daisy and Colonel Boy, are hitched
to the wagon. I hear the cold extravagance of
tiny bells welded into their harness straps.
Iron wheels under us over snow
for miles through the walnut groves. The two
pearled hair combs he gave me
make a chilly mouth on the sill. I look up and out
over water at the horizon — no, two
horizons. One reached and entered with him, and so

is under me, and the other
far enough away to be the dead mate of this one.
Between them, lively passage of boats, none
empty. That's fascinating,
I said to the poet, let me add one. I thought
there was more water in this glass.
I guess not, one of us said.

SAD MOMENTS

That less than torment you lived so fully —
now at least it's possible
to make it functional, the way a chopping block
becomes a footstool once the heads
have rolled. But it gives you no
rest, his holding the stem
of that Japanese maple into the hole
and saying, "Even this thing is going to outlive
me." Tamping the dirt
down with both hands, making sure. Or when,
at the airport in Reno, he came back
glazed over from blowing all his loose change, yours
too — that worse than woeful grin,
cocksure in its lastness, so to smile back was
the less-than-answer needed. "That's the last slot
I'll ever play, I guess." And remembering isn't

to cling, any more than he did, but to acknowledge
no one can die in those moments
either, moments vaulted like a cave with seepage
and echo so they outlive what makes you
forget — those little economies
of the blood that stunt the attention until
the scent of lilac or pitch gets
manageable again and we are fit for modulation and
whim, for cloves and lace, or
that dim creaturely train rushing past us with one
darkened car where nothing but applause
can be heard, and not to know

what it's for, or if its black intoxication
will somehow empty out those raw strips
of night, freshen them
so someone later can lie down for a while,
vulnerable as he was, milder at the end than sleep.

RING

Not the one he's wearing in that stopped length
of ground, but the one we saw together
in the little shop in Oregon — moss agate so green
it was nearly black on its silver band. Hard
to come across it after, emptied of his hand
and watchful. Thinking to surprise its power
with treason, I gave it to our friend who wore
no rings and needed its luck. But soon I knew,
don't ask me how, the ring
lay among lesser things in a drawer. I asked

for it back, and for a while, wore it on a chain
around my neck. But it was awkward
like a high-school charm, the sign of love a girl
outgrows — not as it was, exchanged for the rose-gold
of wedding bands. Where is it now?
In some abject safety.
But where? Put away. I turn the house upside down
searching. Not to find it — worse
than omen. Like happiness squandered in fountains
with wrongheaded wishing. Or the hit-and-miss

taunt of memory, its dulled signature so casual
it crushes me lucid and I believe what I don't believe
in the way of true apparitions — that he uses
my longing to call himself to me,
that my senses are inhabited like the log
into which a bear has crawled to dream
winter away, that the ongoing presence of the dead
is volatile, sacramental. The wind he's

attached to – that boy, running with a kite over
the gravestones, looking up, keeping his footing

as if he worked sky into the earth with
a cool boldness. So the dead-aliveness of my love
turns in the flux of memory, of what his memory
would recall, as he is recalled
to a street in Oregon, dead and alive in love,
with the strangeness of cold silver
close around the finger on his new-made hand.

He Would Have

To speak for him is to leave a breath
pulled suddenly from an overlapping realm
suspended in the room. So this morning
snow lightly cupped in salal is raised against
the hillside by fresh ardor alone
because he would have called to me
while putting on the morning coffee
to look out and see it into its island moment,
spiraled double and darkly inward
by our pushing pleasure up another notch
until the world stays as beneficent as it is.
I stand at the window the better to amplify
cool underneath of petals a snow-lit green.
Any unexpected bounty adds him like seasoning
to the day, as when the eagle uses the frayed
sky-green of the neighboring hemlock to
beguile our paired attentions, his white head
at its topped crown washed clean of the past and
                              the future.
                              Alert raw knot of infinity.

THIEVES AT THE GRAVE

Now snow has fallen I have been to you
in all weather, especially lovebird weather,
a valence throughout, thanks to
the viewpoint at the cliff edge
where teenagers park to rehearse in daylight
certain suppressions of desire
so as to repeal them more aggressively
at dark. Their glances along the shore below
and farther out at the fishing boats reflect a gauze
of homecoming as when your patina of green
wears through me. Purposeful

then to bury you above our fishing grounds.
Purposeful as fish locked in their fluidity,
as we are. Location, says the snow,
is what you do to me, what I record briefly
and change into second nature. My knee-marks
are two bald companion moons where we glide
grassily in place. I leave things
to test your company – the two potted plants
so tempting in August bees were a fever
in goldenrod and I could think, "He loves
their industry." By September someone
had hefted them away into a secret garden.
That simple desecration, the thief's prerogative,

joined you back to my living, and we are benefactors
to shepherds, blind walkers, a braille of winds.
What the bees took they gave again

to flowers as much caressed as we were.
But those glassed-in kisses
with their motors running are edged
by another snow: how did we live so well before
with nothing missing?

COLD CRESCENT

Walking idly through the shops on the wharf
while waiting for the ferry to take us
across — we don't know yet
you are dying. But I hold that black shawl so long,
admiring lace against flesh, the way it enhances me cold
like bird song over snow, partial
and what we vanish from. So you were unafraid and
offered to buy it for me. And neither of us
noticed overmuch as money was paid
and into my hands it was
delivered, a simple swath of cloth.

I remember taking it freshly
out of the drawer, the crispness of black, its
breaking off at both ends into daylight, as death
breaks us off or shouts into itself
until a tingling ambushes the room and it is all we can do
not to follow that swoop of not-coming-backness.

But I'm past that now, as the crescent moon says
of its full stony profile. Tonight the moon is blond.
His sideways light bends inward to cheat
the dark. That's why he's here, to hand me
the white shawl knitted beside some missing fire.
When he sets it across my shoulders
I am lowered gently down
and made to sleep again on earth.

By daybreak a north wind has shaken
the snow from the fir boughs. No disguise
lasts long. Did you think there were no winds
under the earth? My Tartar horse prefers
a north wind. Did you think
a little time and death would stop me?
Didn't you choose me for the stubborn
set of my head, for green eyes that dared
the cheat and the haggler from our door?
I've worn a little path, an egg-shaped circle
around your grave keeping warm
while I talk to you. I'm the only one
in the graveyard. You chose well. No one
is as stubborn as me, and my Tartar horse
prefers a north wind.

III

THE VALENTINE ELEGIES

In love longing
I listen to the monk's bell.
I will never forget you
even for an interval
short as those between
the bell notes.

IZUMI SHIKIBU

*Ink Dark Moon: Love Poems by On no
Komachi and Izumi Shikibu, Women of
the Ancient Japanese Court*
translated by Jane Hirshfield and
Mariko Aratina

Black Valentine

I run the comb through his lush hair,
letting it think into my wrist
the way the wrist whispers to the cards
with punctuation and savvy in a game of solitaire.
So much not to be said the scissors
are saying in the hasp and sheer
of the morning. Eleven years I've cut
his hair and even now, this last time, we hide
fear to save pleasure
as bulwark. *My dearest*—the hair says as it brushes my
thighs—*my only*—on the way to the floor. If the hair
is a soul-sign, the soul obeys our gravity, piles up
in animal mounds and worships the feet. We're
silent so peace rays over us like Bernice's hair
shaken out across the heavens. If there were gods
we are to believe they animated her shorn locks
with more darkness than light, and harm
was put by after the Syrian campaign, and
harm was put by as you tipped the cards
from the table like a child bored
with losing. I spread my hair like a tent over us
to make safety wear its twin heads, one to face death,
the other blasted so piteously by love
you throw the lantern of the moment against
the wall and take me in with our old joke, the one
that marks my northern skies, "Hey, babe," you say
like a man who knows how to live on earth. "Hey,"
with your arm around my hips, "what you doing
after work?" Silly to ask now if the hair
she put on the altar, imagining her power over
his passage, was dead or living.

QUIVER

I am even younger now than you, for a while,
in the way his early death has scraped away my future
so I have nowhere else to go but back, back
to youth, my schoolgirl heart! How it likes to leap, to
throw itself away, tossing the heads off
pansies from a height to let the butterfly come out.
"What more?" it asks, not "how
long?" "Take off your blouse," he says in his hilarious
English, your cardiologist friend from Prague. "Miro,
say *unbutton* your blouse, please." Already he bends — "They're not
easy, these buttons." Such
a beautiful word, *buttons,* when he said
it. Glad for lace to reward him, Miro with his ear to
his stethoscope to my heart, my breast-beat. We are not

twins tonight — you on the couch with your faulty pulse.
Mine is hiding out, refusing to
click. It knows time has no arrow, only suddenness and
yearning, its savage two-edged smile transfigured by
command. I hand you the ivory chopsticks — my hair tumbles
down. It always does when I drink sake, when my hands go
China white. So it isn't remembering, but silver and exact
when I tell Miro of my lost jazz-playing friend, lost
in Prague Spring in 1968, Milosz who loved to kiss
standing up with his hands against my shoulder blades, Milosz
who did not hitchhike to Paris, but disappeared into Prague as a
stone enters well water, though he sent recorded Christmas carols
the second Christmas we never saw each other again. Love gets

younger like that, remembering what didn't happen, younger
and more uniquely desolate, the way youngest love
wants to be rid of ornamentation, to shed, to clasp, to stroke
the wrong way until the skin roars. Miro, whose sleep
I have stolen in my vague lethargy of rain-held
amours, armors, my graceful hinges. What
can he think, snapping his fingers and dancing alone
in the cramped bedroom to the radio's callow
vigor, as we put the book of the moon aside so its crescent
wavers in its cycle of harvest — vessel in which
the shadow of the rabbit is drowned, in which a shuddering
moves its whimsical bohemian soul across the sounds made of

me and I am younger than you have ever been, like a shelter
built from branches by children who will wade the river
and forget, carrying their snowy elbows
like rudders through the current with their mouths
open, as mine is open, and his lips not even lips
they are so far from living, my hair parted
at the neck where his eyelids close, so moonstone, so
borrowed from what I knew of that innocent heart, ghosted now.
As this is kindness, not love, to let the girl
have something to replace, to replay
like false acacias or an artificial lake. Still as luxury
she keeps and keeps, and is a grove carefully
worked upon.

Fresh Stain

I don't know now if it was kindness — we do
and we do. But I wanted you with me
that day in the cool raspberry vines, before
I had loved anyone, when another girl and I
saw the owner's son coming to lift away
our heaped flats of berries. His
white shirt outside his jeans so
tempting. That whiteness, that quick side-glance
in our direction. We said nothing,
but quickly gathered all the berries we could, losing
some in our mirth and trampling them
like two black ponies who only want to keep their backs
free, who only want to be shaken with
the black night-in-day murmur of hemlocks
high above. Our slim waists, our buds
of breasts and red stain of raspberries cheapening
our lips. We were sudden, we were
two blurred dancers who didn't need paradise. His shirt,
his white shirt when the pelting ended, as if
we had kissed him until his own blood
opened. So we refused every plea and
were satisfied. And you didn't touch me then, just
listened to the cool silence after. Inside,
the ripe hidden berries as we took up our wicker baskets
and lost our hands past the wrists
in the trellised vines. Just girls with the arms of
their sweaters twisted across their hips, their laughter
high in sunlight and shadow, that girl
you can almost remember as she leans into the vine,
following with pure unanswerable desire, a boy
going into the house to change his shirt.

Rain-soaked Valentine

As if some child, unwilling to shut even
the figurative heart into pocket or
lunch pail, had carried it plate-like
home in a downpour. A passionate
migration — no matter its redundant shape
and thirty others just as crude. The passage
did it good, white lace bleeding, the stock
message smudged out of language by rivulets
and soaring. It came with a lunge,
earnestness of moment, refusing
to be merely "sufficient" as in prudent love —
the effect gauged before the gift.
Anciently worn to trash on its way to me, it
doesn't care if I am moonlight. Just arriving
is candor, is courting.

CRAZY MENU

Last of his toothpaste, last of his Wheat Chex, last
of his 5-Quick-Cinnamon-Rolls-With-Icing, his
Pop Secret Microwave Pop-
corn, his Deluxe Fudge Brownie Mix next to my
Casbah Nutted Pilaf on the sparser
shelf. I'm using it all up. Chanting: he'd-want-me-
to-he'd-want-me-to. To consume loss like a hydra-headed
meal of would-have-dones accompanied by
missed-shared-delight. What can I tell you?
I'm a lost proof.
But something eats with me, a darling of
the air-that-is. It smacks its unkissable lips and
pours me down with a gleam in its unblinkable eye, me —
the genius loci of his waiting room to this feast of rapidly
congealing unobtainables. Oh-me-of-
the-last-of-his-lastness through which I am gigantically
left over like the delight of Turkish

Delight. Don't haul out your memory vault to
cauterize my green-with-moment-thumb. Or shove me
into the gloom-closet of yet another cannibalistic
Nevermore. I've been there. And there too. It was not
unusual — that bravado of a castrato in a brothel
yanking his nose and waxing paradisal. No, I'm more like
a Polish miner who meets a Chinese miner at a
helmet convention in Amsterdam. Because we both
speak a brand of Philip Morris English picked up
from a now extinct murmur heard only impromptu
at a certain caved-in depth, we are overwhelmed by
the sheer fact of meeting and we clasp

each other by our bare heads for nights, exchanging
the unimpoverishable secrets of the earth, the going down and
the coming up, the immutable pretext of light, a common history
of slumped canaries, of bereaved kinfolk, of black-lunged
singers and handmade coffins. We trade
a few eulogies and drinking songs and sit down at last to
a huge meal of aged cheese and kippers.
We lean into our vitals

with all the lights off. It's dark inside and out.
This is our last chance to revel in the unencumbered
flickering of Balinese tapers we bought at
a souvenir stand above the canal. Like rice and spit
we are tolerant of all occasions, this being
the lifting of the dread whereby
the girls' wings we autograph onto our duffle coats
have been painted like butterflies, only
on the upside so the dark is mocked by
our raised arms, our fluttered concentration, uncollectable as
the lastness I am of him I love-ed
scribbled unsentimentally on a valentine in 1983:
  To the King of my Heart!
In daylight we pick up our tinned rations and hike off,
every artery and nerve of us, into the rest
of our commemorative lives.

POSTHUMOUS VALENTINE

You want me to know I'm keeping memories
so you unlatch a few. The future's
in there too, badly restrained
like an actress so intently fastened on
her cue: "pocketknife" — she stumbles out
on "doctor's wife" and, mistaken
for the maid, is chased out so as not
to interrupt the kiss. But that's already in
the past. I remember how nicely stingy
they were — streamlining my impromptu
intervals like a serious canoe just
composed enough for two.

Strange Thanksgiving

I don't know anyone at the table except
the friend who's brought me, who knows only
the host and hostess. I perch on my chair
like an egret, snowy and attentive. The man
to my left is the youngest son of an onion farmer.
The crop this year was ruined by rain.
His wrist is speckled blue from painting his
girlfriend's Chevy last night. We talk
about his hobby, building underwater cars. He
drove one off a dock into a lake. Nice
to putt around under the ducks, then wheel
on shore and go for burgers. Our host

draws up a chair, offers three kinds of pie.
He plays vicious squash to stay ahead of his bad
back. His wife will be near-dead
on the bathroom floor from swallowing pills
a few short nights away. But things
are holding now. Even that crumb at the edge of
my friend's mouth. I reach up
as if we're man and wife and brush it
away, unconscious tenderness letting my hand
graze for a moment my own love's face
and so, submerged, fall heavily to sea in the homely
clatter of plates lifted suddenly

away. We're stalled out and anxious
in the chitchat before the hearth. Soon
into our coats and thank-yous. Getting to the car
down a fresh bank of snow, I steady myself
on my friend's sure grip. The ride home is better

than sleep, initialled over with afterthoughts we speak
out loud in that half-heard, half-said way—yet easy
to feel rescued by his debonair steering through
the unacknowledged coma of side streets. His intimacy
to know I'm beyond accompaniment and already
home, dividing myself with approach
like two moon-bright windows, seen after dark, across a field.

There is threat of you here as the sea
shows its blackest hour before nightfall,
then doubles back to take it all.
But for a while the trees are silhouetted
against a band of shaggy lavender across
a bridge of pink-edged light.
I could still believe the door will open
and you will be standing there,
a little surprised I'm not with
anyone yet.

Now the light's extinguished
and we who knew every curve and dip and scar
must claim each other like hands picking orchids
in the dark. We can tell only by the fragrance
how much needs crushing.

MAGENTA VALENTINE

Today my love feels Italian, reminiscent of
blood spilled between the Austrian and
Franco-Sardinian armies at Magenta, bluer and
deeper than Harvard crimson. Captain Caprilli is
yet to be born to instruct the cavalry.
The rider is still an encumbrance to the horse.
I drink espresso in the little cafe with its back to
the harbor, try to think of you with other
than longing, more like a very old and mostly forgotten
battle that haunts a few leftover war brides
who eventually married somebody living.
My heart surges blackly. Knows other likelihoods.

Its beak is red and it has a battlefield-look,
as if it's had its pickings and come away
of its own volition. Elsewhere the Emperor Frederick
sleeps on, guarded by ravens, and may yet rise
from deathly slumber and walk the earth.
Who knows what's long enough
when death's involved. I stand on my love's grave
and say aloud in a swoop of gulls over
the bay, "I kiss your lips, babe," and it's not
grotesque, even though the mind knows what it
knows, and mostly doesn't. Language,
that great concealer, is more than generous, gives
always what it doesn't have. I stare into the dazzling
impertinent eye of the messenger. He's
been tending the dead so long his eyes are garnets,
his wings cracked open to either side, two
fissures savage with light. I bend
in recognition and take up a holly bough left
as in the old adornment of doorways. The hard, red
berries glisten and tremble in their nest of
green, so when he speaks I hear him
with the attention of a red berry before a covetous
bright eye, and what I need I take
in empires before he flaps away on my love's errands
and I am cinnabar and fog in the doorway.

I V

And this holy man of great directness
and simplicity, big white teeth shining,
laughs out loud in an infectious way
at Jang-bu's question. Indicating his twisted legs
without a trace of self-pity or bitterness, as if
they belonged to all of us, he casts his arms wide
to the sky and the snow mountains, the high sun
and dancing sheep, and cries, "Of course I am happy here!
It's wonderful! Especially
when I have no choice!"

PETER MATTHIESSEN

The Snow Leopard

PARADISE

Morning and the night uncoupled.
My childhood friend
who had been staying awake for me, left the house
so I could be alone with the powerful raft of his body.

He seemed to be there only for listening, an afterlife
I hadn't expected. So I talked to him, told him
things I needed to hear myself
tell him, and he listened, I can say "peacefully,"
though maybe it was only an effect he had, the body's surety
when it becomes one muscle. Still, I believe I heard
my own voice then, as he might have heard it, eagerly
like the nostrils of any mare blowing softly over
the damp presence he was, telling it
all is safe here, all is calm and yet to be endured
where you are gone from.

I spoke until there was nothing unfinished between us.
Since his feet were still there and my hands
I rubbed them with oil
because it is hard to imagine at first
that the dead don't enjoy those same things they did
when alive. And even if it happened only as a last thing, it
was the right last thing.

For to confirm what is forever beyond speech
pulls action out of us. And if it is only childlike and
unreceived, the way a child hums to the stick
it is using to scratch houses into the dirt, still
it is a silky membrane and shining
even to the closed eye.

EBONY

I need these dark waves pulsing in my sleep.
How else make up for the pungency
of that carnation's breath freshened over us,
night on night? Just to lie next to love
was to have the garden in all its seasons.
I see that now. Gently, and without
the false lustre of pain meant to tempt
memory into crushed fragrance.
In the pull and toss of stones below the house
a soothing spirit sifts and laves its weights,
and those that were tears in some oriental legend
are strongly effaced in the wearing. You,
who were only a stone, taught stone to me in aftermath.
Which is to mock containment at its rich periphery.
The gray, the green in my black.

FATHOMLESS

The peacock has eaten the poison orchid
and shakes poison into beauty of feathers as
easily as my hair unlatches its
black hairpins into the pool
the sunken grave has made of him.
They drop and drop.
From a long way off I hear them strike bone
that could be eye-socket or pelvis or
sternum. The sound is not what I
expected. Not the startled gold
of his wedding band. Not that. More
the soft plinging of arrows shot
in a dream toward my own face, stopped there,
above a pool where someone else's tears
have broken unruly, and fall softly
through the eye.

BREEZE

Don't you think I'm tired of tragedy?
It's not even my word. Not theirs either
when they apply that ghost-talcum
to us. We're comic-strip. Kill one
of us and a legion of lovers
steps forward. You spring to life because
what else can I call it when you
soar into me like a cheerleader marooned
in a meadow. I shake my crepe tassels.
How happily they rustle, tossed there
on the tall grass.

DEAF POEM

Don't read this one out loud. It isn't
to be heard, not even in the sonic zones
of the mind should it trip the word "explosion"
and detonate in the silent room. My love
needs a few words that stay out of
the mouth and vocal cords. No vibrations, please.
He needs to put his soul's freshly inhuman capacity
into scattering himself deeper into
the forest. It's part of the plan that birds
will eat the markings. It's okay. He's not coming
that way again. He likes it where he is. Or if he
doesn't, I can't know anything about it. Let
the birds sing. He always liked to hear them
any time of day. But let this poem meet
its deafness. It pays attention another way, like he
doesn't when I bow my head and press my forehead
in the swollen delusion of love's power to
manifest across distance the gladness that joined us.

Wherever he is he still knows I have two feet
and one of them is broken from dancing.
He'd come to me if he could. It's nice to be sure
of something when speaking of the dead. Sometimes
I forget what I'm doing and call out to him. It's me! How
could you go off like that? Just as things were
getting good. I'm petulant, reminding him of his promise
to take me in a sleigh pulled by horses
with bells. He looks back in the dream – the way
a violin might glance across a room at its bow
about to be used for kindling. He doesn't
try to stop anything. Not the dancing. Not the deafness

of my poems when they arrive like a sack of wet
stones. Yes, he can step back into life just long enough
for eternity to catch hold, until one of us
is able to watch and to write the deaf poem,
a poem missing even the language
it is unwritten in.

We're All Pharaohs When We Die

Our friends die with us
   and the sky too
      in huge swatches, and lakes, and places
         we walked past, just going and
            coming.
The spoons we ate with look dim, a little deadened
   in the drawer. Their trips to the mouth
      forlorn, and the breath caught there
         fogged to a pewtery smudge.

Our friends die with us and are thrown in because we
used them so well.
But they also stay on earth awhile like the abandoned
   huts of the Sherpas on a mountain that doesn't know
      it's being climbed. They don't fall down all at once.
         Not like his heart
fell down, dragging
the whole gliding eternity of him out of sight.

Guttural and aslant, I chew the leather sleeve
   of his jacket, teething like a child on the unknown pressure
      budding near its tongue. But the tongue
         is thrown in too, everyone's who said his name
as he used to be called
in our waking and sleeping,
   dreaming and telling the dreams.
      Yes, the dreams are thrown in
so the mystery
   breaks through still wearing its lid, and I am never
      to be seen again
         out of his muslin striding.

If this is my lid then, with its eyebrows painted on, with its
stylized eyes glazed open above the yet-to-be-dead ones, even so
    a dead-aliveness looks through
        as trees are thrown in
           and clouds and the meadows under the orchards
the deer like to enter — those returning souls
    who agree to be seen
        gazing out of their forest-eyes
with our faint world painted over them.

V

One day a monk came to the master, Yoshu, at a monastery in the mountains. Upon arriving, the monk asked: "This place is very well-known for its natural stone bridge that is said to span the rapids, but as I come here I don't see any stone bridge. I see only a rotten piece of board, a plank. Where is your bridge, pray tell me, O master?"

The master now answered in this way: "You see only that miserable, rickety plank and don't see the stone bridge?"

The disciple said: "Where is the stone bridge then?"

And the master answered him: "Horses pass over it, donkeys pass over it, cats and dogs, tigers and elephants pass over it, men and women, the poor and the rich, the young and the old, the humble and the noble, Englishmen, perhaps Japanese, Muslims, Christians; spirituality and materiality, the ideal and the practical, the supreme and the most commonplace things. They all pass over it. Even you, O monk, pass over it."

DAISETZ TEITARO SUZUKI

The Awakening of Zen

"Said Jesus, on whom be peace: The world is a bridge, pass over it, but build no house there."

Inscription on Akbar's Gate of Victory

Moon Crossing Bridge

If I stand a long time by the river
when the moon is high
don't mistake my attention
for the merely aesthetic, though
that saves in daylight.
Only what we once called worship
has feet light enough to carry
the living on that span of brightness.
And who's to say I didn't cross
just because I used the bridge in its witnessing,
to let the water stay the water
and the incongruities of the moon to chart
that joining I was certain of.

SPACIOUS ENCOUNTER

What they cut away in braids from childhood
returns. I use it. With my body's nearest silk
I cover you in the dream-homage, attend and revive
by attending. I know very little of what to do
without you. Friends say, "Go on with your life."
But who's assigned this complicitous extension,
these word-caressings? this night-river
full of dead star-tremors, amazed floatings, this
chaotic laboratory of broken approaches?

Your unwritten pages lift an ongoing dusk in me.
Maybe this makes me your only reader now. The one
you were writing towards all along, who can't put down
her double memory pressed to shape
your one bodiless body. Book I am wearing in my night-rushing
to overtake these kneelings and contritions of daylight. Book
that would be a soul's reprisal
if souls could abandon their secret missions
so necessary to our unbelief. No,
the embrace hasn't ended.
Though everyone's grief-clock
runs down. Even mine sweeps
the room and goes forth with a blank face
more suited each day to enduring.

Ours is the compressed altitude
of two beings who share one retina
with the no-world seared onto it, and
the night-river rushing through, one-sided,
and able to carry what is one-sidedly felt
when there is no surface to what

flows into you. Embrace
I can't empty. Embrace I would know with my arms
cut away on no street in no universe
to which we address so much unprofound silence.
I unshelter you—my vanishing
dialogue, my remnant, my provision.

ANNIVERSARY

If the sun could walk into a room
you would not dare to want
such a man as he. But blindness
has prepared me, is requisite
to love put away, like breath
put away from the half-opened mouth,
breath that returns, withdraws,
returns again. As he does
and does not.

We ate the wedding feast quietly
and to ourselves near the hush
of the gaming tables, the icy click
of dice in the half-closed hand
before they are thrown.
There were no toasts to the future
because by then it was a day
about to begin, which
was already stunted
by the hazard of its own
oblivion. What could I tell you
of love at that moment
that would be simple and true enough
since words are candles I blow out
the moment I set them down?
Better to scrape wax from the table edge
with a fingernail. Better to stare
into the eye of a horse
brought to drink from the mouth
of a river where it opens
into the sea. All was liquid

and tranquil there, and though our lips
were kept from touching
by the great sleep of space
before us, everything poured into us
hard and true, and when we set our glasses
down, the darkness of the horse's
overflowing eye closed over us.

to fold the clothes. No matter who lives
or who dies, I'm still a woman.
I'll always have plenty to do.
I bring the arms of his shirt
together. Nothing can stop
our tenderness. I'll get back
to the poem. I'll get back to being
a woman. But for now
there's a shirt, a giant shirt
in my hands, and somewhere a small girl
standing next to her mother
watching to see how it's done.

CHERRY BLOSSOMS

Chekhov wanting to write about "the wave of
child suicides sweeping across Russia" – plunged
by that sentence into sudden pity for
myself and my three brothers growing up,
as my father had, under the strap. Pity
for my father who worked and slept, worked
and drank and was the dispenser of woe.
Our child bodies learning despair, learning to quake
and cower – the raw crimson of pain given by
the loving hand. No wonder, for a while,

animals drew close to us, as if our souls
overlapped. And so we died there. And were
attended by animals. One dog especially
I remember with brightest gratitude.
Miles of night and her wild vowellings under
great moons, subsiding into a kind of atrocious
laughter, what I think of now as faint gleams
of demoniac nature ratifying itself. Somehow

that viewless dread she recorded seared
my childhood with survival – she who
was mercifully and humbly buried somewhere
with a little *sotoba* over her, bearing the unnecessary
text: "Even within such as this animal,
    the Knowledge Supreme will enfold at last."
                    And so my old friend died.

And the cherry blossoms fell sumptuously.
And I wrote a little *sotoba* in my determined
        child-hand, to insure that never again
could they be put back
               onto our bare branches.

KNOTTED LETTER

*It seems to me, though, that you
always understand very well what I
can't say very well.*

HARUKI MURAKAMI
A Wild Sheep Chase

There is that getting worse at saying
that comes from being understood
in nuance, because the great illiteracy
of rain keeps writing over my days
as if to confirm the possibility
of touching everything so it glistens
with its bliss bent aside by some soft
undirected surpassing.

I say to the never-injured creature:
the shears have rent my silk – unsolving
beauty, hard and bright – until I am so consequent
with time it is accomplice
and spills neither backwards nor
forwards. I ask him to live by miscalculation
my capricious scheme. Counsel him to miss light
an oar's moment and be ocean-cold
as love's splashing after-touch, the blade-edge
actual, but under spell
and scarlet to what it gladly slips
as a thing too near and precious – a shadowy fish
drowsy with the overgarment of planets and stars
it haunts below, as if to commemorate
the unseen by the marbled distortions
guessed at. Because the kisses come mixed with sand
and we know the mouth is full of strange, unwieldy
sediment. And because the samurai image of a sword

is thrust through clouds with only the hilt
showing, its unglinting edges like words
slashed to stubble where the wheat was gathere

And this a gleaning twisted to the leafless bush
he was sure to pass, thinking by memory
her waist-length hair, her spoken face
as he would never see it, in the words
of poems so keenly obscured
the poem was her only face.

I Put On My New Spring Robe

Yamato Takeru-no-Mikoto, samurai hero of the Kojiki,
who "turned into a white bird upon his death."
No accident then, the headstone
to your left reads "White" and the one chiseled
to your right is "Bird."—A man who could arrange this,
not knowing where he would be buried, has to be scary.

I burn cones of incense and watch the sweet smoke
drift across our faces. Yesterday when someone
asked how I was doing I laughed
like a woman whose fate is to sleep next to a sword.
Whitebird, that's what I call you in my dreams of flying.

Our stones are subtle here, a lavender that is
almost gray, a covert green
a step shy of its blue.
For eating, as with loneliness, we prefer
the bowl to the plate, for its
heaping up, its shapeliness of offering
what it half encloses. Just
when it seems the day has gone to sleep, the eagle
drops suddenly from its black chambers.

The silks of drowsy weddings sham the horizon and ecstasy
is a slow mirage we drift towards, voyaging in
some eternal orient whose seasons
ache, serenely inhabit, but disdain
to yield. The *she* who rules here leans
across the void to reward our perpetual suspension
with an ongoing tomb – "If," she says, "you
existed." Requiring pleasure to revolve
outside its answer.

Picking Bones

Emiko here from Tokyo in her red dress
and voice like a porcelain hand
on silk. We carry roses to the grave
under the tilt of gulls. Some have
walked their hieroglyphics across the poem
carved there, to make sure we comprehend
this stopping off to flight. Small tasks

prepare another silence, kinship of pouring
water, fallen petals brushed across granite.
Gradually we come there after we've
come there. Hard to light candles
in the breeze from the strait. His delight
flickers and gusts. We are steady
and erased a little more. Finally we talk quietly,

the presence palpable as we crouch there.
That overlay too of new sound Emiko has given
his poems in Japanese. Our voices nudge closer
on the cliffside. Pungency and sweetness
of joss sticks, Emiko says, in Japanese cemeteries,
and smoke curling up. After cremation of the loved one,
working in pairs, the relatives join in the ritual

of "picking bones." Two by two with chopsticks lifting
each bone from the ashes, dropping it
into an urn. Her friend, Yoshi, who said he had
much feeling and grief on viewing
his father's body, but who saw and felt,
in lifting shards of a father – the lightness, the necessary

discrepancy of translation. For a moment we are held
precariously as a morsel
on the way to any mouth. "Don't
pick bones!" the mothers warn children caught
lifting the same piece of food. We pull
ourselves up from the low black table, from

                              the ivory clicking.

BLUE GRAPES

Eating blue grapes
     near the window
and looking out
     at the snow-covered valley.
For a moment, the deep world
     gazing back. Then a blue jay
scatters snow from a bough.
No world, no meeting. Only
     tremors, sweetness
          on the tongue.

AT THE-PLACE-OF-SADNESS

I take a photo of the stone Buddha
gazing from its eternal moment over
the eroded bodies of hundreds of child-sized
Buddhas. Shoulder to shoulder
they say something about death
not to be offered another way. The spirits
of those with no relatives to mourn them, an entity
driving tears inward so the face wears only the gust,
the implosion of grief.

Through the starred red of maple leaves: a man
half-visible in white shirt and black tie
held on a level with the stone Buddha—the one
in its living stillness, the other more-than-living
so he takes a step toward me
when I press the shutter
and glance up
like one of the dead
given the task of proving, with two identical stones,
the difference between
a spirit and a body.

Hefting turf onto the cart
in the long light, Helen's son Ricardo
gone home. Sufficiency of women's arms
in that old necessity of wars and rain. Mary
stacking the load as we swing the sacks up – good
use of knees to boost the heavier ones
into place. The air still and
brackish, pulling us close
on the hillside. Angela, forgetful in her
silk blouse, brought to the work
so suddenly her white is magnet to the scuff
of earth, the heels of her palms, like ours, etched
with the fine black of secret fire
the earth had been saving.

We ride the bonfire to the cottage yard
to stack the winter's heat. The flickering red
of cockscombs yet to bloom brushes the tractor wheels
to either side. How light
the earth is between us. Strange we are
in the blue air that stores its night.
Strange, like figures crowded off the edge
of memory.

CLOSE TO ME NOW

Through low valley mist
I saw the horses
barely moving, caressed flank
and forelock, the dip
of the back. Human love is a wonder
if only to say: this body! the mist!

INFINITE ROOM

Having lost future with him
I'm fit now to love those
who offer no future when future
is the heart's way of throwing itself away
in time. He gave me all, even
the last marbled instant, and not as excess,
but as if a closed intention were itself
a spring by the roadside
I could put my lips to and be quenched
remembering. So love in a room now
can too easily make me lost
like a child having to hurry home
in darkness, afraid the house
will be empty. Or just afraid.

Tell me again how this is only
for as long as it lasts. I want to be
fragile and true as one who extends
the moment with its death intact,
with her too wise heart
cleansed of that debris we called hope.
Only then can I revisit that last surviving
and know with the wild exactness
of a shattered window what he meant
with all time gone
when he said, "I love you."

Now offer me again
what you thought was nothing.

Two Locked Shadows

Their joining is the way a buried self
exerts its chill in order to ravish
the greater light around it.
Like me, they cannot see what love loses
in being useless, but can feel
its certain gain. I will be poor
as darkness is to night
watching them in my soft hunger.
Where does her shoulder end or
the blue sparks thrown off
by his chest begin? My eyes
make up their grandeur
from a shapeless swelling, a clashing
without movement
that belongs to happiness
and signifies: only the body
is generous, is strong enough
to live past the sugary, hunchbacked claims
of the soul. The double cinch of
their sex draws my stepping through
like a sudden dart of pain
or joy, impossible to know which,
since whatever happens, when I step
into sunlight, they have kissed
my white cheekbones
expressionless.

GLOW

Those Japanese women waiting, waiting
all the way back to Shikibu and Komachi
for men who, even then, seemed capable
of scant affection. Traitorous though,
not to admire the love of women
that shines down long corridors of the past
as steadily as those lanterns
I walked under beside the shrines of Kyōto.
Women who waited in vain, or to have sorrow
freshened by a cursory reappearance.
Their hope of meeting even a poor love again
gave each heart its rigorous vanishing.

Even a beautiful waste is waste.
Someone should have stepped through
the cobwebs in their pitiful doorways
with a new message: "Not the work of love
but love itself, nothing less."
That at least might have emptied
them sufficiently
to carry expectation past
its false chance at fulfillment.
Which is to say — when no right love came
they would not have been ready.
Something close at hand
would have claimed their attentions.

So I walked out one night under the full moon
and agreed with my dead love
that the cold light on the backs of my hands
belonged most to me.

VI

He holds me. Rainbows everywhere. What is more like a
    rainbow than tears? Rain, a curtain, denser
than beads. I don't know if such embankments can
    end. But here is a bridge and
                               – Well then?

MARINA TSVETAYEVA

Selected Poems
translated by Elaine Feinstein

Light begins. Snow begins.
A rose begins to unhinge
its petals. Sleep
begins. An apple lets go
of its branch. Someone tells
a secret like an echo
wrapped around a shadow,
a shadow soaked in love.
The secret begins to make
a difference. It travels
on the borrowed heat
of what the shadow
passes over. The lip
begins its mustache.
The heart begins its
savage journey
toward love and loss
of love. But you, you
don't begin. I stare
at your hand on my breast.
Their dialogue is the wingless
strength of the stem
bearing its flower
in rain, in sun.

Day begins. Night begins.
But you don't begin.
You know that one thing
the loveless lovers forget,
that to begin is to agree
to live among half-forces,

to shine only when the moon
shines and all is ready.

You make me ready
but you do not begin.
I let you never begin.
It's my gift to our most uncertain
always. I agree only to coincide
outside each death-enchanted
wave. What we are making
isn't a shroud or a halo.
It's a banished hive
stinging itself alive with
vast multiplications. We taunt love
as the bullfighter taunts
death, preparing the dangerous lunge
until it catches us unawares
that split second
in which love shudders
its starkest glimpse
into us. The magenta cape
swirls its silk across our lips
like a breath unraveled in the moment
the matador kneels to the bull.
My *adorno, el novillito*. Don't
begin. Don't ever begin.

INCOMPREHENSIBLY

*Because we have chosen them
those who had no reason to be braided
in moonlight
are bound together.*

My friend is back from Cairo.
He is tired in the eyes from all he has seen,
and tired too from drinking whiskey straight
in the little dusty cafes, keeping up with the company.
We drink a little whiskey to join one far midnight
to another, and because my black-haired orphan
is with us. She whose brown eyes
have added a crackling to the night, whose body,
lithe and brown, came somehow to rest
for swift years near that of my brother.

But for a night within the smell of mountains
we are sisters another way, and her glances, black butterflies
of the general soul, join me to one
who is missing, who sleeps like a hive of wild honey,
who sleeps with his sweetness
intact like a blue door sure and firm
in the swift corridors of the night.
He who tries to wrest shards of love from the world
in broad daylight, who loves only a little
at first, then madly. "Love,
such a run-down subject," said the ancient poet
of Rio. My orphan smiles and clicks
her whiskey glass to mine.

In Cairo the camels throw the weight of their haunches
onto their knees and raise up. An old man passes through
the cafe swinging from a chain his brass cylinder embossed

with stars and half-moons. The charred droplets of burnt musk
rain over us, seep through our sleeves onto our skin.
My friend is talking about his Italian motorcycle.
Love, such a run-down subject, especially,
forced as I am, to mix these living creatures
with ghosts, haughty with the axe-edge beauty
of a woman's indifference, with the sleeping lips of that one
who lies even more deeply asleep in me
like a trail of cut flowers from my doorstep to his.

Suddenly the bar is noisy, the music
a raw throb at the base of the brain. We can't talk about love
or anything else in here. Time to put our arms
around each other's waists—my man, my woman, my
unapproachable dream. Time to walk out
into the pungent streets of Cairo with kisses of good night
on a street corner where it is dark and cool enough
for weddings that happen all night long
to the frantic pulse of the tabla. Move back, the men
are dancing, the men are showing their sex in their hips, their
bellies and waists. The rose water is splashing our brows
on this street corner, unappointed as we are, but bound inexactly
by whiskey, loud music, Italian motorcycles, by the unknown
parents of my orphan.

And in the wide silence of each step, the implosive blue rose he
dropped unknowingly into my thigh
keeps alive love's ache, love's incandescent whisper
under the black smell of mountains. And I don't know why
we are together, dear ghosts, or why we have to
part. Only that it is precious and that I love
this run-down subject.

I Don't Know You

And you don't know me.
Out of this the loudest appeal
to harm or advantage.
Don't move. I like this ledge
of loose diamonds waiting to be spilled
into the night. Let's shine awhile
without touching. Sensuality is,
after all, a river that is always waiting.
Let's wait another way. Not for
anything, but because waiting
isn't a part of nature. I don't want
to take a step toward death
in anyone's company, not even
for love's sake.

I like how you know not to speak.
If I could arrange a true moment
to startle us into a right communion,
I would have a small boy come toward us now
with a bowl of rainwater.
It isn't for us. We're as unmysterious
to him as rain falling into
rainwater. He puts his lips to the rim
and drinks, but not without seeing us.

So history is made of unconscious glances
threaded by the unreapable memories
of children. But stay a little longer
unconfessed to me as a kiss
we agree to forswear. I love
this slow carriage, the heavy bellies

of the horses, the harness which
has scraped me down to hide.

And now I know you less
and you will never know me
as one reduced by the casual
or even the half-closed eyelid of desire.
That way is ancient but, like twilight, a sign
of elements overlapped against their wills.

Ours is another luster,
as if a soul had died outside the world
and divided itself in two
in order to prepare the lucid, intricate pleasure
of its welcome.

Yes, let's agree also
not to believe in the soul.

Tame love that remembers a birthday
but scorns the every-moment,
how you robbed the pit from the cherry,
that wooden pearl I was carrying
under my tongue. Talisman
of silence wedged between the poet's words
when I say, "Don't you know
I'm the joyful girl inside
the woman with the forever-melting ghost
on her lips?" If the word "happy"
has a future it's mine because
I don't exist in the favored shell
of what I'm meagerly given. Isn't
there enough sky? Isn't there
laughter and running? Can't the ardor
of one smiling face make a deer leap,
even when to leap could mean
an alternate calamity?

I have only these hot-cold widow's hands
to touch the world back with.
You know that and it doesn't stop you.
Something sacred, a vast accord between
my ghosted-love and how it could
convey the shadow-selves of some happiest
surrender — was this
what brought you?

Be equal to it then, like a deer that chooses
to leap over a rose. Like a rose with its leaping
above it.

THE FOREST SHE WAS TRYING TO SAY

Tonight I feel compassion for everyone,
those who are pitied, along with those who
are kissed.
MARINA TSVETAYEVA

The angel wings of the hemlock
aren't for flying. They are the fragrant arms
of a stately spirit held in the shape
of an unlived moment when the world,
in all its woe and splendor, disappeared.
To visit the sunless core
of the forest is to say to the heart,
which is always a remnant, "Love as if
you will be answered," and in that fiction
to force love wide
as the invisible net of bird flight
between the boughs. Here tenderness
has squeezed light to infusion.
Why is love so vengeful and absent
because one diamond kiss
fell out of his mouth with sear
intent against my throat?
Did he mean never to be thought of apart
from love? Angel, those wings
aren't for flying but in defiance
of all that harsh traffic
on the soulless plain. This
is the forest, or at least a small
forever-kneeling wood. And we are adorned
and adored here because we wear the gall

of an impossible love.
Angel, don't look at me like one
cast out and piteous. This is Eden
and the gods are elsewhere. Angel,
we will be thrown out. We will fall
down and be that other wild.

How well he knows he must lift out
the desolate Buddha, unfurl the scroll
raked anciently with its dragon's claw
of waiting. Silk banner embossed
with the myriad invigorations of the blood
pulling the tide toward us
until our bodies don't hoard eternity
but are spun through with a darting vehemence,
until the abundant thing made of us spikes free
of even its ripening, that moan of white fingers at a depth
that strips the gears of the soul.

I lick salt of him from under his eyes,
from the side of the face. Prise open each wave
in its rising, in its mouth-to-breast-to-groin.
A velvet motionlessness where the halo
lingers as if between two endless afternoons
in which a round presence, most quiet and
most unquiet, is tended. Because love
has decided and made a place of us.
Has once again asked its boldest question
as an answer.

We are the lucidity of salt, jealous
even of its craving. It follows
its thirst with its neck outstretched
so like the shy deer
who come down from the mountain.
They run their quick tongues
over the wet ribbons of seaweed. But we are so far inside
the body-ness of the body, that the hieroglyphics of their hoofprints

inscribe the many-paired lips of the sea's cave mouth
which, even now, drinks wave onto wave.

We are overspent into awakening like the pinched scent
of aniseed that carries its sex
as a bruising. He lifts himself like an answer
in which love, as it knows not to speak
but is many-chasmed, says, "Ask me. Ask me
anything." Again, his palm passes over
the mute belly, passes and repasses.
Her gold and silver rings in a heap
on the headboard. His naked hand. Hers
more naked. The sea turned back nightlong
by the blackened tide of her hair
across no shore.

Kisses from the Inside

He has invented a way of guiding
the blind woman so they can step exactly
together. As she is not led, so is he rapid
and ingenious with me. I am like a house lost
in the woods of Soto
whose upper floors are occupied by gypsies.
They braid red yarn into my hair
and light my shadow with candles to keep me
all in light. He wants me all in light,
she who was stumbling three years
with the dead. He picks my feet up
by their heels in his palm. The more
I want to be high and golden, pitiless and
unformed, the more he tears me back
to earth. He rolls me in the red dust
inside the night. Even his kisses
stroke my unwinding from the inside.
The bees fly off from their honey,
their unspeakable frenzies.
In the hovering noon of our devotional midnights
he flies off, until I am sheer and stolen,
rooted deep in the sea air
          because the tide is everything
                    because the tide is everything
and I have never seen the sea.

A Light that Works Itself
into the Mind

If the fish could only half-swim
like an agreement to be half-in-love
the vision of its divine fluidity might hesitate
without comfort, without being consumed. But
it must plunge in freedom-light, luminous and
natural as the language of passersby, yet imprecise
enough to keep a true identity. Light
that is a dwelling or a road that still enters
where someone has fled and forfeited a joy
from that day on. By the open window
she is braiding her hair and thinking what to give
amply, while his flesh unlives itself,
urgent at the rim of her slow unreasoning.
Where has he learned to turn back pleasure
like an almost-summer? And what does it mean,
this something lighter-than-himself
he renews in her like a letter read inside out
because its own listening asks something to be told
away from the very moment of its outward light?

Like a child's freshly kissed face
only the honest heart is free, is able
to return its dazzling to the starry, open land.
Everything he fears to tell her is like an image
that pierces the painter's canvas
from the other side. And it stays on her fingertips
as a spider-climb of heart-constraining wonder
long after his wave to wave
has worn away his mouth, the wet sacramental voice
that had been their most silent body.

If This New Love Ends

To love is to accept that one might
die another death before one dies one's own.
MARIANNE WIGGINS

Someone to follow him? I don't think so.
It is like proposing a second heaven
as if it were attainable because you played
with angels in your childhood and believed
in the wings of their flesh.

A young girl strokes the tight braids
of her hair and thinks she is one memory.
A little eye gleams in moonlight
hoping to be freed of its love of water, of
foggy nights, of wings tangled
in the hair of celestial heads.
I would die again for that girl
who received everything the world suggested
as if each moment were an ascension.

But I have used up my deaths in loving him
as he died. And if this new love ends
it will have to go on in me
like a mountain behind a town
when the mountain is made to watch that town
enter flames and smoke
until it at last resembles the essence of love,
that impersonation of his heart's heart
which, one day in the girl's second memory,

became a little eye in moonlight
where he lived in her, imperishable
as anything offered to coexist
with the unreplaceable.

Near, As All that Is Lost

Don't play it like it's love.
It's a memory of love.
The conductor, FRANCIS TRAVIS,
instructing the volunteer orchestra,
Tokyo, Japan

What are we now, who were two unsynchronized eyelids
lifting the day-into-night world beyond its fictions
of life forever? One eye watched
the other eye in its unbound search for a way back
to a language equal to the dream-washing of our past,
that all-severed pledge each death falsely requires.

I couldn't allow the day-star behind the night-star
until another life leaped over
the beautiful rubble memory hid in me.
Now love is my joy-injured orbit like a bow
drawn by an arched wrist across two strings of a cello
and above this, the listening hand
bending one of the notes as pain-in-transit bends
language to purposes outside meaning.
Only then can it hide its resonance
in new love's shadow-drinking.

Such joining bewitches, and not through harmony,
but through a stretching of memory as we don't know
how to speak its sensations, but must play them out
as bodies, as if the wishfulness of the soul to feel
would come into us, as it comes, as it does come.

And now the shadow takes a step for
us. And I speak into the shadow
its love-name, its most tender body: *Morenito, Morenito.*

So it walks for us and lies down for us and polishes
our one body of light, the one that slides over the earth
like a black platter with the world on its shoulders,
with its feet under our feet.

NOTES

TOGETSU BRIDGE : "Moon Crossing Bridge" is a translation from the Chinese characters for the Togetsu Bridge, which spans the river Oi near Kyōto in the Arashiyama area, known for the many important literary works that celebrate its beauty. In the days of the aristocracy there was a fanciful custom called *Ogi-nagashi* of floating fans down the river from boats.

The mountain area on the Sagano side of the bridge is also known for its many temples and as a retreat area for those wishing to take up lives of solitude. As I walked across the Togetsu Bridge in late November of 1990 with two Japanese friends, it occurred to me that I had literally just walked across the title of my book.

The name of the bridge is said to be an allusion to the moon crossing the night sky.

PAGE 65 : *sotoba* – A long, narrow wooden tablet set up near a grave, inscribed with a sentence from the Buddhist sacred books, and the name of the deceased; supposed to facilitate the entrance of the soul into paradise.

PAGE 83 : In the lexicon of bull fighting, *un extraño* is the sudden deadly lunge a bull can make. In common usage, *extraño* is an adjective meaning strange or odd or foreign.

PAGE 84 : An *adorno* is the kiss or touch a matador sometimes gives the bull as a sign of respect before the kill.
el novillito – little black bull.
Morenito – little dark one.

PAGE 94 : In "Kisses from the Inside" the woods of Soto are near where Federico García Lorca was raised in Andalusia.

ABOUT THE AUTHOR

Tess Gallagher's previous publications include *Amplitude: New and Selected Poems, A Concert of Tenses* (essays on poetry), and *The Lover of Horses and Other Stories.* *Portable Kisses* (poetry) is forthcoming from Capra Press in April. She lives in Port Angeles, Washington, where she has recently completed the introduction to *No Heroics, Please,* the first of two volumes of *The Uncollected Works of Raymond Carver*, edited by William Stull.

This book was designed by Tree Swenson.

It was set in Monticello type by the Typeworks

and manufactured by

Edwards Brothers, Inc.

on acid-free paper.